Family Light .

Shining light on the poetic voices of families

Rose
Wellbeing
Therapies
TO FLOURISH FROM BIRTH & BEYOND

First edition:

ISBN 979-8-662-64829-6 (Paperback)

Book Design by Rachel Kirkpatrick

Published by Rachel Kirkpatrick, Founder of Rose Wellbeing Therapies

~

Dedicated to the poetic voices of
Family

~

About This Book

This book is a collection of poems from the heart & light of families about love, birth, longing, mental health, loss, family and lockdown. Written in 2020 when the world went into lockdown during a global pandemic.

"Only when we are brave enough to explore the darkness will we discover the infinite power of our light"

Brené Brown

Contributions

Little Miracle

Precious one,
So small,
So sweet.
Dancing in on Angel feet
Straight from Heaven's brightest star

What a miracle you are!

Well my Son, Nathaniel, what can I say
You brighten up my every day
What a surprise you were to me
But such a little miracle, you see

Rachel Kirkpatrick

Elentiya

Once you were just a star in the sky
That I hung every dream, every wish,
every hope on.

So, if you ever doubt your strength,
beauty or place in this world,
Please remember that you have
Stardust in your veins
Moonlight in your soul
And the sun's radiance in your heart.

You could never be confined by worldly ideas
like princess or even warrior.
You were born to blaze across the sky.

Everything is possible for you my love.

Eppie Sprung

Away into The Wind.

Away,
into the wind,
taken weightless
without wings

To turn the clouds,
to toil the seas,
to gather leaves
from sleeping trees

To be the breeze
against the glass
and help the falling snow
to dance

You sing to me
I watch the tide
you touch the tears
I cannot hide

Through my fingers
cold you flow.
I hear you hush
and whisper low…

I breathe you in
and try to hold…
I breathe you out
I let you go.   Emma Gillespie

Sunflower & Fox Cub

A Poem to our Son & Daughter

We prayed for you,
Our beautiful sunflower
For what seemed like the longest time
The universe heard our prayers,
And soon we were blessed with sunshine

You filled our life with so much love,
joy & meaning
We thank our lucky stars every day
We decided to pray once again,
And soon a little fox cub came our way

Our house is now filled with laughter, laundry
And treasured memories to keep
Life is now, both busy & calm,
With moments of chaos & beauty together

You have blossomed &
your petals radiate the sun,
And our fox cub is growing
adventurous & wild like heather

Both beautiful blues with soft beach blonde hair
One shy, sensitive & creative
The other curious, loving & runs without care

Unique & precious are all of your traits
We love watching you grow & develop
Changing with each coming day,
And becoming such good mates

We aren't sure if our little family is yet complete,
But we are happy & trust the universe to decide
Becoming parents is our greatest achievement,
Our little sunflower & fox cub
You fill our hearts with such pride

Stay wild beautiful babies.
Trust in the universe to be your guide
Some things may take longer than you expect,
But the wait is absolutely worth it

Love Mummy & Daddy xxx

Shelley Gibson

It takes me some time

Don't call me slow.....
I take things at my own pace
Still with a long way to go

I have to work harder than most
Things are not as easy for me
Spend a day in my shoes
Then you will truly see

Please don't compare me
You will see I won't be beat
One day it will happen
I will walk on my feet

In the meantime, I will battle on
Learning new things every day
What my parents show and tell me
They show me how to play

Delayed development is just a phrase
It's like waiting for a clock to chime
So, they put a label on me
Who cares, I'll do things in my own time

Carrie McFadzean

I'll try my best

I'll try my best for you my boy
I don't have much to give you
Mummy's on her own you see
But never forget I am always here

I will say though, if I say no to you
It does not mean that I don't love you
Or that I wish I could always say yes
Always remember, money is not all

But what I can give, is all my heart
And with all my strength I'll try
I'll cuddle you when you cry
I'll kiss you every day to say goodnight

What I will do forever more
Is pay you all my attention
I'll mend you better when you fall
And I'll hold all memories deep inside

If you are ill, I'll play nurse
And when you perform, I will be proud
I will take you on holiday far & wide
The photos taken will be treasured

When you are cold, I'll keep you warm
A clean & happy house I'll provide
With meals & baths & really fun times
Family & friends will surely visit us

As you get bigger, I'll watch you grow
A happy chappy, many a friend you will make
I'll tell you every day how much I love you
A Mummy's boy, so pettied
You can snuggle in my bed anytime

Although I'll worry & over protect
I'll try my best to give you space
But don't forget to tell me your woes
I shall be to you a trustful friend

You can make mistakes but always learn
I'll stand by your choices Son
Rest assured and make each day its own
I'll try my best to be your Angel

For you, I give my soul, my everything
My Son, My Angel, My Nathaniel
I am so proud of you my Son
And will forever be proud to be your Mum

Rachel Kirkpatrick

A Poem for my Mummy

Lemons are yellow, limes are green
When I see your face
I think it is supreme

Apples are red just like a rose,
Or when your beautiful
Cheeks are cold

I know I am not the best child,
But don't blame me if your
Voice is so Loud!

But in the end, you love me
And I love you back, but more
Than you do to me

Before this lovely poem ends
I wish you will always love me
Until the world ends

Lexi Reid (Age 11)

Being Dad

The Midwife said "it'll be a while,
why don't you get some air"
The aroma from the hospital kitchen
was more than I could bear

Sausage, egg, bacon and beans,
what a way to break my fast
After such a long, long night
my hunger's gone at last

I take some air out in the grounds
and rest upon a seat
Then wander casually back inside
to find the delivery suite

The Midwife's busy when I arrive,
it's all a bit of a whirl
Then she hands me a little bundle,
"meet your baby girl"

The love is instant, the bond complete
Two tiny hands, two tiny feet
My heart could burst, my tears do fall
My pride and joy, you are my all

A few years later and your sibling's due
His birthday planned, the date we knew

He's rather large, in the wrong position
A selective 'C' Section, the right decision

We get a chance to choose his birthday
The 8th of January, we'll go for Friday
The fact I knew but chose not to tell
It's only Elvis's birthday as well

The 'C' Section's done, your brother's born
Through the viewing glass you and I look on
No chance to hold him, see his tiny feet
But once again the love's complete

For more than thirty years I've been a Dad
A choice I made of which I'm glad
No words can describe a Father's love
It amounts to more than heaven above

Les Kirkpatrick

An Ode' to my Auntie Dana

Well my Auntie, what can I say
As you dance, prance and sing too
I will forever watch you with fascination
And look up to you

You make me squeal as you tug and pull
And if you get too close, I'll try bite you
But as I grow tall and strong
I will get you back with all my might

Dana, my Auntie, my friend
I love you dearly my guardian angel
You can always come stay with me
For memories we will share, forever and a day

Rachel Kirkpatrick
Written for my Sister from her nephew Nathaniel

About my Buddy Dog Simba

When I was 8 years old, I got Simba,
When he was a young dog
He had to have an operation because
He was injured

He used to be a guide dog then,
He became a buddy dog for me,
Because I have Autism

Irvine Currie

Safety in Solitude

Pacing the comfortable confines
of my peaceful prison,
Such familiar walls continue to creep
Drawing ever closer as I shuffle aimlessly along,
Carpet wearing thin under exhausted feet.

Blindly sleepwalking through endless lazy days,
While my soul dances with
Spirits through the night.
Curtains drawn as a new day breaks,
A beautiful bubble of chaos, safety, and
uncertainty.

So far removed from a life once lived,
No thrill, no purpose, no commitment.
A tiny shell lies beneath soft sandy sheets,
While ferocious waves continue their deafening
roar.

Sasha McMurtrie

Locked In

Tangled
Cornered, Confined
Restless, Frantic, Clawing
Locked Inside my Mind
Ensnared

Violet McMurtrie

<u>Monroe</u>

You were born on a sun soaked
Seturday efternoon.
September wis the month,
Dumfries the toon.
We couldnae believe oor eyes,
You wur here,
Oor miracle, oor prize!
You bloody well took yer time,
But hey, tak nae heid, that's nae crime.
Skin tae skin we kissed an cuddled
As the midwives muddled an guddled.
September the 6th 2014,
The best thurs been!

Daniel Gillespie

An ode to my Love

We are different.
So different.
We are alike.
So alike.
Then we aren't again.
And so on.
And so forth.
We've had conversations about this
And wondered if it is too different at times.
No, it is not.
It is beautifully imperfect and
Beautifully us.

Nicola Cloherty

Son

Sometimes a just watch you sleep,
Cuddled intae the nook o' ma arm.
A could sit like this forever an a time,
Watching o'er ye, free fae harm.

So peaceful, you drift aff tae sleep,
Aw ma troubles vanish an ur gone.
These times a feel very precious
But they'll soon be done afore too long.

But fur noo, a take it aw in,
Each day, a day at a time.
We roe, your ma wee man,
You ur perfect, you ur mine.

Daniel Gillespie

You

The moment I met you
I just knew in my heart
That we shared that spark
And since then, never apart

Funny, kind and handsome are you
I think I loved after date two
Laughter, Love & Light
I knew I had to hold on tight

To the man of my dreams, yes you
A tough mudder, rough runner & a meal or two
Remember that night you lost a tooth
Eating pizza in our private booth

I never knew, until I met you
That there was another bond so true
A boy & a man come together to play
So natural to you, the fathering way

I sometimes see myself in you
Alike we are, soulmates so true
You hold my hand & play with my hair
To lose you is something I could not bear

In my heart, it will always be you
Please never fall fixing a flue
My dreams come true, when a home was ours
To decorate for hours & hours

Stuck in Lockdown with you
And our home & love grew
Drills & banging & stripping the walls
All for the plan of a beautiful hall

Games, walks & cycles with you
And many a picture that we took
Secret walks with many a green tree
As the world was waiting to be free

The best of memories is always with you
In Rome & Turkey we loved the view
A cold caravan & hidden heat revealed
To festival fun & a yurt in a field

More memories I want to make with you
Maybe one day a vow or two
More plans and travels with three
And dragged along for a shopping spree

Don't ever forget, it will always be you
My heart will always be pure & true
And I'll never stop asking when I need to
Can I keep you?

Rachel Kirkpatrick

Little Boy Blue

In March I found out I was carrying you
I couldn't wait to hear the word pink or blue

Things got off to a bumpy start
With fluid round your neck and a possible bad
heart

After some weeks you got the all clear
My beautiful boy I couldn't wait to hold near

The 21st was when you were due
So excited to meet my little boy blue

On the 24th as I slept, you were kicking away
How could you be gone the very next day

Going into hospital I could barely breathe
For my baby I would have to grieve

I had some time but to the angels you would fly
My little boy blue in the playground in the sky

Lynsi Mills
D&G Baby Loss Awareness

Uplifting

In the lockdown I have thought a lot
As the weeks go by still the news is a lot
No news is good news, so they say
I am waiting for something else they'll say

I wait patiently for the light
Let's draw a rainbow with colours so bright
My home is a safe place
but my husband still works
So, we follow the rules as they do work

We get separated from family
And friends for a while
But one day soon we will reconcile

The boredom kicks in but hey
We stay in a beautiful place I do need to say
Mountains & fields in the countryside so perfect
Staying in touch with loved ones is so perfect

My strength is uplifting
I surprise myself
By uplifting everyone else

I have learnt a lot
From being locked up
Now let's wait and you will see
A whole new world for us to see

Kelly Malone

While You Were Sleeping

While you were sleeping
One moment it's normal and
Then things happened fast,
Who was to know that time would be the last?

While you were sleeping
The world kept on turning
Things carried on
The rudeness of the world too
Not recognise you were gone

While you were sleeping
Others fortunate got to share,
Or have a groan
How dare the lucky even think they could moan?

While you were sleeping
I battled with illness,
I battled hard times
I overcame loss and looked for the signs

While you were sleeping
Movement flooded in,
 Things began to change,
Situations and times grew very strange

While you were sleeping
I gave in to feel the pain
I allowed myself to accept
That nothing could be as good or as perfect

While you were sleeping
I communicated to you,
I met you in my dreams,
When I awake, I realised all is not as it seemed

While you were sleeping
I missed you. I loved you,
I wished you were here,
I would have done anything to have you still near

While you were sleeping
Life began to happen,
Such events that it brings
I often wonder what you would make of such
things.

While you were sleeping
I have stayed awake,
Knowing there was more for me
In this world still to take

While you were sleeping
I became a mother,
I became a wife
I learned a lot and progressed with my life

While you were sleeping
I hope I did you proud
One day we will meet you again and,
Soar through the clouds

Lorraine Roxburgh

One day at a time

Can I make it through another day
Will you ask me how I am
Will you wait to hear the answer
Will you even give a damn

Should I talk to someone close to me
Will they pick up if I call
If I say I'm really not ok
Will they even care at all

Would they notice if I cried for help
If they saw me shed a tear
Would it be the best for everyone
If I wasn't even here

All these things go through my head
Every day & every night
And then one day I made that call
And darkness turned to light

They listened to my every word
I knew that come what may
They'd put their arms around me
And I knew I'd be ok

Did they see I was a mess
Did they love me, did they really care
When I asked they all said yes

Can I make it through another day
Do you even give a damn
Don't be scared, just be friend
And ask me how I am

Claire Jordan

Special Moments

I wish I could remember those newborn days
The endless cuddles and nighttime feeds
The countless full nappies that I couldn't change
The complete lack of sleep that I found so hard

Now you have changed and grown so much
Your personality has blossomed & developed
You smile at my face & laugh at my silly face
You sleep on your own & chat happily to toys

You are such a special and wonderful being
I look at you countless times every day and
Count my blessings with every glance
I cannot believe that I made and
Carried you inside me

You will change and grow more and more
Things you will learn and people you'll know
I can't wait to be by your side as you develop
Don't change too quickly, you have much to
Conquer and time goes so fast

The person you are and the person you'll be are
all very special to me

Rebecca Barnard

Friendship Poem

You may meet a person and instantly know
That you will be best friends forever
Other friendships develop
over an extended period of time

In some friendships you may feel
A sense of equality,
While in other there may be a clear sense
That one is giving more to the friendship
Than the other

There are no rules about
how a friendship has to be
If you are able to share your life
With another human being,
By all means go right ahead

All friendships are unique
And special in their own way
Each one is valuable

I just want to let you know
That we really appreciate
You coming into our lives
And being there for us

You definitely know how to make us smile
Whenever we are feeling down
Our friendship means a lot to me
And we love you
From the bottom of our hearts

Anne-Marie Jordan

Time Out

God knows everyone needs
A little coaching now and again
He gave us the gift of free will
To choose which way we want to go

He knows everything about us
He has been by our sides from the start
And when we get confused or broken hearted
We tend to carry our burdens and pain

We carry them like a heavy load
That drags us down into despair
God calls time out for us to be still
And hear his voice

To stop what we are doing and take time out
To reflect and listen to what he
Is telling and showing us

For his help and forgiveness
And then forgive ourselves
And others who do us wrong

Because when you serve others
With a whole heart and humanity

You serve him also

God loves his children endlessly
No matter what they do
And like any other Father
He only wants what is right
For me and you

Grace Brown

An eternal memory of sadly missed sisters

To lose someone as dear as you
Brought sorrow and much pain
And I'd give everything I have
Just to see your face again

For you were really wonderful
As special as could be
And I miss you so much because,
You meant a lot to me

But all the love I have for you
Will never go away and sister dear,
I do believe we'll meet again someday

We all sadly miss you both
And wished you were all here
With us laughing and giving us cheek,
As we all miss it

Lisa & Karen are always in our hearts forever….
Love you both so much

Anne- Marie Jordan

If only she knew the steps

Crisp autumnal footsteps
Through a child's shout
The glee echoed by decades of time
Now open a rift of falling memories

The location sits like a painting on a wall
Unchanged, yet standing here much has past
Stilted words uttered by convenience
Underlying an orchestra of hate

Unbeknownst to the lamb the knife is falling
Holes appear in the painting and
the ducks take flight
No gold adorning, now stands a girl
Reduced, rejected but not forgotten

Steel teeth clamp tight around a wavering tear
Bright light appears before her
Blowing the painting wide
Stepping through, a hand grips, then another
A staircase of arms carry her on

Rising through an enveloping cloud bank
To glimpse the ocean

Two small hands clutched tightly to her side
Through a child's shout
She echoes it through the decades of time

Angela Nixon

I shed a tear today

Right now in fact, as I stand barefoot
Looking out at the water that stretches
To the left and right; as far as my eyes
can see.
I'm listening to the water hitting the shore. It's
calm.
The sun glistens on the water with
a chill in the air.
I shed a tear.
A tear for this freedom we've taken for granted.
A tear for Mother Earth we've ignored.
A tear for those alone right now.
A tear for incredible humans working
and fighting for lives while risking their own.
A tear for all the souls struggling in fear.
A tear for the past me.
A tear for the truest me.
A tear for who I am to be.
Shedding tears is releasing and appreciating and
opening and connecting.
Do not be afraid to shed a tear today,
or any day.
You are but human.
With a heart full of love.

Nicola Cloherty

2020!

We need to stay strong,
It seems all has gone wrong
There will come a day,
It won't be that long,
The threat will pass,
We'll all be free, at last!
Until the darkness is past,
Keep safe to the last

Jo-Anne Griffiths

Rainbow of Emotions

We have a rainbow of emotions
Red can be the feeling of anger
Yellow can make us feel bright
We may hide behind pink cheeks when shy
Envy can make us green
Orange is the colour of courage
Calmness flows with purple
Tears may fall when we feel blue
We all have a rainbow of emotions

Karen Gibb & Rachel Kirkpatrick
Adapted into a poem from a Story Massage

Three Hundred and Sixty Five

My boy, today you are one.
Happy Birthday to you
Another day spent in lockdown
but then that's nothing new

I'll make it extra special and
we'll have lots of fun
Especially for you my Button Moon,
because you are second to none

You keep me laughing all day and all night
Being a family of three has never felt so right

I watch you learn, I see you grow
You are more special to me
than you will ever know

Three hundred and sixty five days
of being your mum
And Heath I have loved them, every one

Mari Glendinning

Watch this space

Early morning, sleep evades,
The excitement and anticipation
too much to bear
The journey to the bathroom,
Test in hand, is quickly over
The wait feels long, so long

Bleary eyed, I look down,
A white stick waiting to predict the future.
'Even a faint line is a positive'.
Time is up... there's a line.
Wow - it's happened, and fast!

A busy day ahead before,
I can check with another test.
A day of singing and dancing - in my element,
Watching my cast enjoy their final show.
Crackalacking, so crackalacking. So proud.
Pregnant 1-2 weeks - it was right!

Then it hit, March 2020 - the virus.
Robbing some of their loved ones,
the air they breathed,
The chance to see their friends and family for
months on end

Our baby is growing amid such unusual times,
His dad unable to see him at the scans,
His mum unable to access midwife support in the
usual way...
but we are all here and we are healthy.
Thank goodness

As we watch baby grow
through my expanding bump,
We don't know what the next few months hold.
We hope our baby enters the world with less of a
threat to the human race

We continue to plan and watch him grow as the
future unfolds- watch this space!

Sarah Hubbard

The best sister

Imagine having a best friend since birth,
That is what having a big sister is like,
Rachel is the best sister anyone could ask for

Kind & caring, and just wonderful in every way
She is helpful to me every day
We have been on holidays together in the sun
Loch Lomond was one and we had so much fun

We drank some tea and ate sugar cubes
And spent our days walking along the beach
A trip to Legoland in Windsor, near London
The weather was no good,
but we still had a good time

Many a day trip from here to there
Face painting festival in Blackpool
And nothing is better than when we squeal
At the pleasure beach, many a times

Oh, the shopping trips to Primark,
Going out walks and hikes, but not in the dark
They're even better when we get lost
So many times, we've been out to lunch
So many places, it's hard to decide my favourite

This year we were due a trip to Spain,
Then there was corona, such a pain
Into lockdown and sad to not see her

But now I can see her again once more
And it feels so much better
She's the best sister anyone could ask for
And I wouldn't want her any other way.

Dana Davidson

<u>Teenagers</u>

Stereotyped, misunderstood,
I still don't and I never could
Understand why all parents are told
"Just wait 'til they get old and take themselves off
to their bedroom or cave, and stop talking,
grunt, or generally behave like no one can
possibly understand what they're experiencing
in their new-found land"

They almost act as though,
When they were small
Their big emotions weren't met at all
Instead when they'd overload and start to shout
Their parents would put them in time out;
Their emotional literacy hushed to a sum of,
"When you've calmed down then you can come
out"

So, what do our children do;
What do they learn?
That unconditional love is something to earn?
That it's ok for Mum & Dad to have a bad day
But if they have one, they should hide away
No wonder then, when they become a teen
With polarised feelings and nothing between,

They start to impose time out for them self
Choose silence & park how they feel on a shelf.
All anyone wants is to feel they've been heard
To be validated, listened to, each single word.

When teenagers start to be met with respect
When we see their potential qualities, are yet to
be discovered gems valued & rich,
Then perhaps we will see their true purpose and
ditch the negative stereotypes, an adult behest

So, parents of young ones,
Thinking this age is the best,
Please don't wish away the years,
Enjoy the cuddles and the fun
But don't regret the pace of life;
The best is yet to come

Catherine Jackson

My best friend

When I was just 3 years and 10 months
The best surprise ever happened
I was told I was going to be an Auntie

The only thing I remember is walking in the
hospital doors
I felt like it was my job to protect him
Nathaniel is one of the best things to ever
happen to me
I couldn't imagine my life without him

Lockdown has been so hard
But we have been on FaceTime so much
And I get funny Snapchat's from him
Our socially distanced walks aren't quite the same
But that way we can still see each other

We have been so many places together
We've been to Legoland, Blackpool pleasure
beach, Loch Lomond
We've also been camping a couple of times
They always end with sore stomachs from
laughing

He's taken me on walks I've never been before
I've taken him places he's never been
We are always up for an adventure

no matter what the weather
He's taught me many things
Some include football and
how to build the best dens
He doesn't like it when I beat him
at football though
I've taught him how to do my makeup
He's still not mastered that very well though

He's watched me dye my hair with lipstick when I
was bored
And I've watched him grow up to be the funniest
person ever
His jokes will always be the best
Even the ones he told when he was young

Our water fights are elite
You know it's getting serious when the blue
gloves come out
When he was younger, he used to cry when
I splashed him with water
Now he just gets me back bigger and better

He's my best friend forever
And I'll always look after him
He can always count on me
I wouldn't change him for the world.

Dana Davidson

Goodbye Poem

I can't believe the day has come
The time to say goodbye,
It seems just like yesterday
that you greeted me with Hi!
This year hasn't been the way
We hoped for it to be
With COVID causing havoc & causing us to flee

Home learning has been the norm
Since March the 23rd
Sumdog, Spelling, grammar, grids &
Learning about birds
I wish we could be together in class,
Just one more time
To fill the room with laughter &
Know that everything was fine

I will treasure all of the memories
Each and every one
From Dukehouse Wood to Opera,
This year was so much fun
Remember when we danced to Thomas &
Sang to Bruno Mars
These were such special moments with you
My P6 stars!

I adore each and every one of you
So special and unique
I couldn't have picked a better class
And wish that we could speak
I've watched you grow & blossom
Into the role models that you are

This year you will all be buddies,
Georgetown's superstars!
I'd better say goodbye now but,
Don't want to let you go,
I hope we meet again and hope that you all know
I will keep you in my heart &
Remember you with fondness

And wish you all the best
for a great future full of promise

Alison Foss
Primary Teacher

A Parent's Love

A parent's love is a blessing from above
To guide us and to show us how to love
To show us what is right and wrong
To help us grow up big and strong
To prepare us for that eventful day
When we decide to go away
To hold us close when we are sad
To teach us what is good or bad
It's really good to have a Mum and Dad

Our parents are our best friends
Our broken hearts they try to mend
They will wipe away all our tears
All those years they have cared for us
And never really made a fuss
We are glad that they are there
To show us how much they really care
So, we will thank the good Lord up above
For our Mum and Dad's wonderful love

Grace Brown

Sensory Walk

When you go for a walk, what can you see?
Light shining on the leaves of every tree.
Fluffy clouds in the sky above
And rainbows in windows, made with love.
When you go for a walk, what can you hear?
Chatter of families and a cheery hello.
The clatter of footsteps on the ground below.
Feel the gentle breeze and
the warmth of the sun.
Smell the colourful flowers, one by one.
Take time to find joy everywhere
In this sensory world we all share.

Mary Atkinson
Adapted into a poem from a Story Massage

Motherhood

When you were born I felt so many feelings.
I wanted to feel that true rush of love,
Willing it to come.

I knew that I loved you and your quirky ways.
I knew that my life would never be the same.
I knew that our little family was complete.
I knew that my heart was bursting with pride.

I didn't know how hard I would find everyday
I didn't know how much
I would cry at small things.
I didn't know how tired I would feel at all times.
I didn't know how much help I would need all
the time.

Now time has passed and I've learnt and grown.
I realise I needed those times on my own.
I know that my life is fully complete and I love
every moment even those that are tough.
I still have good days.
I still have bad.
I still need to cry for no reason, more times than
you'll know.

Now I have support from family and friends
I know I can tackle anything that

is thrown my way.
The months and the year wasn't
what we expected.
Missing out of so much, me resenting the world.
But you have no plans, enjoy our home time.
Learning and growing with Mummy and Daddy.

The motherhood is here and nothing can stop it.
The motherhood is difficult and
complicated and funny.
The motherhood is here and I wouldn't change it
for the world.

The motherhood has landed and I couldn't be
happier.

Rebecca Barnard

The Love of God

When I look around
I thank the love of God
For all the beautiful things I see
He created them all with love
The birds that fly in the air
He made them all with loving care
The flowers that grow up through the ground
Even the lambs that are leaping around
The fish that swim in the sea
He even created you and me
All these things we take for granted
Even the seeds we have planted
So, if one day you are feeling blue
And you don't know what to do
Just take a look around you
And remember God's Love

Grace Brown

Loss & Light

A poem about losing my Dad & finding my light
again

Being a child was pure wonder & joy,
Running & laughing wild & free.
Protected from all that is scary,
Everything a childhood is meant to be.

Through a child's eyes the world is magical,
Each new day has a million possibilities.
Seeing each new person as a potential friend,
Playing all day with no responsibilities.

Eighteen years old,
the world became dark overnight.
One day you were here, everything well,
The next you had turned out your light.

The pain & sadness overwhelming,
My heart heavy, my throat constantly burned.
The tears seemed never-ending,
Everything in the world was upturned.

It took a long time to feel real again,
I felt like a part of me had gone.

That's when he walked into my life,
The reason my light could shine on.
Some people don't believe in fate,
But some things just can't be explained.
How someone can find you at just the right time,
And your faith in the universe is regained.

He has helped me to heal & to grow
To laugh & to love & to hope
Together we have weathered many of life's
storms,
Holding onto each other to stay afloat.

Each time I am hit with a new loss,
The pain of losing my Dad aches once more.
But I know nothing is promised forever,
I try to treasure each opportunity that knocks at
my door.

We now have our own little family,
That fills our hearts with so much love & pride.
I watch as our children are full of laughter & joy,
And I pray that I will always be around for the
ride.

As I get older, I think of my Dad,
How much turmoil & pain

he must have had inside.
So, I arm myself with self-love & understanding.
Because even with loss, there is always light.

Shelley Gibson

Keep Going

We have made it this far, keep going
I know it's hard, the days are long
But you made it 6 months in
Let's pray for a bit more sun

Outdoors to play & have some fun
I know the stress can feel like a tonne
But you made it 6 months in
All the chores don't need to be done

Go outside and enjoy that sun
If it's gone you will not burn
But you made it 6 months in
We have made it this far, keep going

Rachel Kirkpatrick

Day by Day

Day by day I sit alone
Think of things I have done
And wonder where I have gone wrong
My heart is filled with sadness and woe
Wondering where my life will go
I think of things that come my way
Maybe tomorrow I'll have a better day
No more abuse, hate or torment
No more tears or years of repent
I wander aimlessly on the ground
Jumping at every passing sound
I stand and look towards the sky
And ask the Lord why oh why
Will my heart be free from pain
Will I be able to live again

Grace Brown

5 Little Butterflies

Wedding bells, honeymoon and the future in front of us
Excitement of the unknown awaited us

3 months later, 2 blue lines
Pure joy & happiness as we
Started planning our future.
'I'm sorry there is no heartbeat'
Our world came crashing down
Our hopes and dreams were,
Taken away in a moment

4 months later, 2 blue line
The relief of a healthy baby
Growing bump & butterfly kicks
A beautiful baby girl, just born too soon
Heartache & disbelief

8 months later, 2 blue lines
Hopeful, fearful & afraid
'I'm sorry there is no heartbeat'
Lonely, numb & angry

6 months later, 2 blue lines
A baby boy

Nappies, pram, cot & baby grows
25 weeks & 3 days of loving you
You arrived too soon
We got to spend 6 hours with you
My brave baby boy

You gave me strength to make changes,
Family & friends helped raise money in your
name for families to have a place to go
To remember all the beautiful babies lost

4 months later, 2 blue line
'I'm sorry there is no heartbeat'
Disbelief, anxiety & sadness
Grief doesn't last forever,
But Love does

Lauren Brydson
D&G Baby Loss Awareness

High Hopes

It's said there's an active grim reaper, full of
doom and gloom
And me, I've just never touched the other side of
the moon.
Here lies the plight of a realist, taut now
tenacious dream
A future full of the unveiled and for me
unfamiliar….Perturbing

Destination; journey into the unknown my
forlorn new future
It's just not of this world, limitless residents
reaching rapture.
In our domain all expectations change
to global remains
Airborne altitudes, claim moondust for future
prosperity….Revelation

To elevations beyond this plight, I should take
the next flight
Population of planet earth find restrictions quite
annoying.
Avoid becoming a statistic, it's just some are not
complying

As the grim reaper with you on this globe is not
toying….Affirmative

Dedicated followers of wellbeing oblige, gladly
for a time
At their peril still aid with tears the more and the
many.
It should cherish these, take action from doom
and gloom
Claim for them if I could the other side of the
moon….Yearning

They say it's a persistent grim reaper, full of
future endeavour
Life's frozen in an instant; a minute, remember
the departed.
There's no rhyme nor reason to this
indiscriminate germ
COVID 19's death awaits, freedom from this
reality someday….Expectation

I have high hopes of good coming from doom
and gloom
For Scotland and all surrounding countries
affected.
My future is stay home, stay safe, clap for cares
and NHS

Plan ahead at any rate; dream of cures in the near future....Realistic

Rita Dalgleish

More Space for Love

Like the sounds of the waves
I let things go
Like the whistles of the tree
I let things go
Like the laughter of a child
I let things go
Like a duck to water
I let things go

Nicola Cloherty

Donald

I was a stay at home kid,
Docile, quiet and shy
My family thought I'd never find
Someone on whom I could rely
In my late twenties
My Dad said "We'll get her a wee dug"
With a bit of a shrug
As I'd let time pass me by.

Donald started off as a friend
And quickly became so much more
Husband, Father and Chauffeur.
I love you darling
You're in my corner
When push comes to shove
Someone to watch over me
And for me to Love.

Eleanor Ritchie

A Dream

I have a dream of fame and fortune
I have a dream of love and peace
Sometimes I dream that I can fly
With fresh wind upon my face
Away from war and the human race
Then in the cool light of day
My dreams all fade away
Back to reality to the ground
Drugs, violence, war and hate
You never know what's outside your gate
What can we do to make things good?
How can we get ourselves understood?
Will there be less people unemployed?
Or will the world be destroyed?
All the answers we will never know
So, we will continue to go with the flow
And continue to dream our dreams
And maybe one day they won't be
JUST DREAMS

Grace Brown

Finger Painting

How many finger paintings can you do in a
lockdown?
Turns out a lot
Until you lose the plot
It's a funny thing isolation
It can make you stop
The chaos of life has halted
The daily distractions have decreased
Your mind is now confronting
The trouble with lockdown is not matter how
many finger paintings you do
Your child is there and needs attention
And so do you
So, keep the little ones busy, paint, read &
explore
But look after yourself in lockdown until you can
walk freely outdoors

Candice Torley

Where's the Girl?

Where's the girl who embraces the long dresses?
Who wore make up each day and did her hair?
She enjoyed her weekly weekend spin
And seeing her friends and family.
Things have changed slightly.
She now wears comfy clothes.
Her hair a mess on top of her head,
And her face pale and red.
She now takes daily walks,
And Facetimes her family and friends.
She's confined indoors and working from home,
She struggles with the same four walls.
No break from parenting,
Or time on her own,
She's in desperate need of a break.
She longs for a hug, a friendship embrace,
For barbecues and music with those she loves.
She longs for the beach and walks in the sun,
And maybe five minutes to herself.

Emma Cottam

Our Rainbow Home

A poem of Love, Hope & Hand Gel

Locked up in a rainbow of hope & despair,
Forced to stay in, wash our hands, wear a mask,
Keep away from our loved ones, all to show we
that we care.

Days blend together with no purpose or aim,
Netflix & chill, bake a cake, do schoolwork, clean
the cupboards,
Staying in pyjamas all day with no shame.

Precious togetherness to forever treasure,
Undisturbed family time, playing games
Reading stories, laughing, painting pictures
All the things that bring us pleasure.

All the while the world descends into chaos,
Illness, worry, panic, dying.
Losing loved ones, friends, neighbours,
With so much protection,
There is still so much loss.

A time we will never forget,
Rainbows in every window,

Clapping for carers in every street,
Prayers going out for people you've never met.

Feelings of loneliness & isolation,
Even in your home surrounded by people,
Desperate to reach out, find connection,
Lose the feeling of frustration.

Slowly the world begins to regain normal,
We can finally escape, get outside, breathe again,
Things are beginning to feel much less formal.

Rainbows have taken on a whole new meaning,
One of hope, of loss, of remembrance.
A symbol to remember this time,
Of love, hand gel & Covid-19 screening.

2020 – The year the world went into lockdown,
We will forever have a rainbow in our home.

Shelley Gibson

The Glow

I heard a lot about the 'pregnancy glow'
The light around you as start to show
Body changing, bump defining
The inner workings of life beginning
Hormones racing
Mood swings emerging
The chaos of pregnancy in all of it's beauty
The ups and down of nature engaging

The glow? Where is it
I must have missed it
I had sickness
Headaches
Backache
Heaviness

Come the day you arrived
I caught the first sight
Of a beautiful boy surrounded by light
That was my glow
It was you
It was shining inside
Out of view

Candice Torley

Awake

Awake
The day starts again
Snacks, crumbs, toys - piling up
I want to hold you tight
But I crave space for me.
I want to play with you all day
But I crave a minutes peace.
The days are long
I count down the hours till you fall asleep
And then count some more
till you wake up.
We eat together, we get fresh air together
Then it's time for bed
You snuggle into my arms
You take longer to fall asleep than before
Once you are soundly asleep it is my time
But I am exhausted.
I wonder what tomorrow will bring
I wonder if I'll manage to find the calm and space
I so desperately crave.

Emma Cottam

Our Home

A place where we are never alone,
The foundation to stand on when things go
wrong.
Many pictures frame the walls.
Always here to break the fall.

Through the chaos and the feuds,
Peace is made and all is good.
Courage and strength, swallowed pride,
A bond so strong it stretches wide.

On each other we can depend,
Any hurts we're sure to mend.
The trials and tribulations we always share,
Our home, a place of love and care.

Violet McMurtrie

Otherhood

Childhood to adulthood
Expectations of parenthood
Social norms to be understood

When I was young I loved nature
When I was grown I felt pressure
Childhood to adulthood

Even nature couldn't
Avoid the label
Given to the capable

I felt as maternal as socially acceptable
I birthed a child by my own 'free will'
Childhood to motherhood

I felt love that was authentic
Judgement that was constructed
I desired the empathetic

I reflect on the child
Seeking solace in her ambitions
The ambitions got lost in the otherhood from
Childhood to motherhood

Candice Torley

For the Love of Death

No matter,
How close we get,
Our skeletons
Will never touch.
We will rot together
But be together no more.
Our dust and bone
Will become friends,
Hold hands and
Settle in the earth.
Our love undying,
Our love is real.

Daniel Gillespie

The Bus

Why of all the days in the bus late today?
You'd think it would know
That we are on a day out.
It took three hours to get out of the house,
My mouth moving in constant nag mode:
'Get dressed, Get dressed, Get dressed!',
Our feet tip-tapping into the car to come here
To get to the bus.
Because you are excited about the bus:
It's your special treat.
We climb on, me in mum-mode and you
Desperate to find the first seat you find.
The driver thinks you are a bit weird-
Who could be excited about going on a bus?
But I know. We know.
We don't need your label to excuse your grin
As you climb up onto your knees,
Holding onto Dad for the corners,
Nose pressed to the glass, waiting for the next
traffic light, and exclaiming,
'Look Mum, I'm on the bus!'

Kerrie McKinnel

17/01/10

I can't get you off my skin,
You're in my head
And I've let you in.

You are the power of
A thousand suns.
The river that
Runs through my veins.

Daniel Gillespie

Can we do it again, Mum?

Can we do it again, Mum?
All the things we did in spring,
Those were my favourite days, Mum
The ones where we stayed in.

Can we do it again, Mum?
All the painting, arts & crafts,
Remember the cards I made, Mum?
And those little paper rafts.

Can we do it again, Mum?
Read books and put on a play,
Pretend the tiger came to tea, Mum
That was my favourite day.

Can we do it again, Mum?
Build dens and camp outside,
We danced under the stars, Mum
And laughed until we cried.

Can we do it again, Mum?
Have days where we don't get dressed,
Watch films in our pyjamas, Mum
I thought that was the best!

Can we do it again, Mum?
Play Poohsticks and go for walks,
Ring Nanny every night, Mum
Those were my favourite talks.

Can we do it again, Mum?
Eat together every day?
I loved Dad being home, Mum
He worked but got to play.

Can we do it again, Mum?
Stay up late to clap outside,
Paint rainbows every week, Mum
You displayed them all with pride.

Can we do it again, Mum?
Play games, bake cakes and sing,
I've never felt so happy, Mum
As I did with you that spring.

Liz Binks

Goodnight Blessings Prayer

It's bedtime my little one
The stars are shining bright
The moon will work it's magic
When you close your eyes tonight
You are safe
You are beautiful
You are loved so very much
Now let's get tightly tucked in bed
Sweet dreams & goodnight

Tracey Allen
Adapted into a poem from a Story Massage

Universal Heart

In utero the heart wrestles to find form:
Her two halves incomplete force skin
Pushing boundaries to meet as one: rebirth
Has nothing to with losing or winning.
When wars are over, as in birth: a river of blood
Remains between us.

Fear brings each lamb to the slaughter.
Bleeting never meeting in an emotional void.
In such space: the seed of our loving lies:
Blaming, shaming, as if the other
Could process our pain. Remaining still as
A star cycle we are continues.
Some are called to conquer
Whilst others live in mountains heart.

Where daughter weave in words,
Create in caves, an enslaved art of intuition
Within the ice capped tops which you seek to
conquer lies wisdom of a world at peace:
Turned inside out, stitched up like this darned
sock. Woven for a lovers weary foot.

Careful now: with the knife, the gun, the pickaxe
or the plough.
When you hack the ice around the mountains
heart or tear your country apart.
Remember we are one universal heart
Furiously beating to be whole again

Denise MacColl

Embrace

I want you to come back home.
I've missed you so much.
Just to see you again,
To hear you again.
I've died a thousand deaths
And I'd die a thousand more.
Just to feel your embrace,
One last time.

Proud

Am so proud of ma wee son,
Makes me smile, he's the best, second tae none!
His smile lights up the room
An his laughs escape the gloom.
Fur he is ma wee lad,
Monroe ma boy, am one proud Dad

Daniel Gillespie

Florence

I'm pregnant, let this journey begin
I feel so much excitement and happiness within
Will it be pink, or will it be blue,
Will there be one, or will there be two?

These nine months have gone by so quick
I have felt great, no complaints & not feeling sick
This is it, I am ready, I cannot wait,
It's just the labour now to negotiate.

She's here, she's perfect and she's all mine
I'm so happy, relieved and on cloud nine
Her rosy cheeks, plump red lips & dark hair,
I can't help but feel proud, and sit and stare

We're home now let the journey begin,
But I feel so many mixed emotions within
I am tired, anxious, scared but still proud
All these feelings overwhelming and profound

I feel happy sometimes, but also alone,
But I'm surrounded by people, never on my own.
Is this normal to feel how I feel?
This situation I'm in feels so surreal.

Some days I am full of panic, & feel I can't cope
But wise words from loved ones
give me some hope
There are days I feel I have a mountain to climb,
But I now know this will just take time.

As I stare intently at her beautiful face
The feelings I have start to fall into place
She's a stranger, so helpless and
unaware of her presence
I just need to get know her, my baby,
My Florence

Ellen Burfitt

<u>May 2nd</u>

I watched you turn red, gasping for air.
Without hesitation, I smacked your back

-probably too hard and too many times-

But, it worked, it saved your life!
The grape fell to the floor
As tears ran down all our faces,
My hands were trembling.

You shook hands with death
But we broke up the meeting.

That moment replays in my mind
from time to time,
reliving the panic,
the sheer terror is horrible.

But, you are here, alive and well
And I love you so very much.

Dad.
Daniel Gillespie

Superheroes wear Masks

Superheroes protect
All the people on this earth
Superheroes wear face masks
Just like you and me
I will be like a superhero
When I go out today
Wearing my face mask
Protecting everyone
Superheroes wear face masks
Just like you and me
There will be many superheroes
When I go out today
But! I'm not scared!
No! Not me!
Because superheroes wear face masks
Just like you and me

Tracey Allen
Adapted into a poem from a Story Massage

<u>Life and Death</u>

Life
Is
More
Painful
Than
Death.
Love
Is
More
Powerful
Than
Fear.

Daniel Gillespie

Remember

Remember the year I was born, Mum
The one where the world stood still,
You said we stayed inside, Mum
To keep us from getting ill.

Remember the year I was born, Mum
It sounds like a crazy time,
People wore masks to the shops, Mum
And stood in a two-metre line.

Remember the year I was born, Mum
We never made any plan,
And when we did venture out, Mum
You were always gel-ing your hands.

Remember the year I was born, Mum
My sister was turning three,
You were worried she'd miss preschool, Mum
But she loved it with you and me.

Remember the year I were born, Mum
You gave use extra cuddles
We didn't get much grandparent time, Mum
Until they introduced 'bubbles'

Remember the year I were born, Mum
It was hard but special too,
You might think that we missed out, Mum
But all we needed was you.

So please don't be hard on yourself, Mum
I know you sometimes felt torn,
But we formed an amazing bond, Mum
The year I was born.

Liz Binks

<u>Milk</u>

It was too hot
For a wee tot.
Have it, he could not
He fought and fought
For what he sought,
Wanting the lot,
He was distraught.
Heating up in the pot,
All for what?
MILK…..
That we bought,
Drank the lot
And now not a drop.

Daniel Gillespie

Mother Voice

Do you know the sound of your mother's voice?
Muffled origins
Amniotic resonance
The low rumbling of a steady wub-wub
Heard through the drywall long past being sent
off to bed
Heard conversing with your father in the blue
light of morning
Shouting up the stairs to get ready for school
Don't make me come up there. Get out of bed.
One. Two.

I had walked time's long corridor and heard it
echoing in the halls
Muffled resonance
Amniotic origins
Until I walked that low red hallway long enough
to know it was following me
Familiar tenor, déjà vu tones,
Oh, that woman, doorwoman, ferrywoman,
she carried me over the first canal
Stepped off the dock and she caught
my wobbly legs
As much as time would try to take it from me,
like everything else

Palms cupped over my arms, dulling the light
Hands pressed against my ears,
blocking the sound
It can't rob of the memory of that first voice
Muffled resonance, that steady wub-wub
What other voice do you hear from
the inside of a body
That's building you bit by bit
The sound of creation heard that
voice in the womb
of my first residency
My first and last hermitage
Coming down the corridors, echoes of the flesh
laughing, talking, singing, crying,
That ready thrumming, that steady wub-wub

Do you know the sound of your mother's voice?
I grew up my whole life in the South
That wet womb, humid corner of my country
Spent enough years growing up there
that the world
Could strike me blind and
if I wandered it long enough
I could find my way back just by
the sounds of the South
Hands reaching out in the dark
Grasping at branches of poplar and pine

Do you know the sound of where you were
raised?
The South isn't far from the sound of my
mother's voice
And I'd find them both in the same place
Bullfrogs in the mud
Mountain creek running high
Trees are whirring again, cicadas so loud
I can't sleep
Whole world's buzzing
Soft like treading on mimosa blossoms
with bare feet
And there it was, didn't you hear it?
Just like a clock you can't count on
Summer storm rolling in,
rumbling in from the east

Gutter's overflowing and
I'm trapped in the rain again
Home again
Thunder coming down and
wrapping the whole world in it
That whole wet dome of Southern summers
Under the wide belly of the sky
Until I couldn't tell the difference anymore
between my mother's voice

And that blue shuddering of sound running away
from the light
That low rumbling, that steady wub-wub
And I only knew both from being
Wrapped up in it.

Bryan Maxwell

About this Book

This book was created by Rachel Kirkpatrick, founder of Rose Wellbeing Therapies. I support Mothers, Babies and Toddlers in the small town of Dumfries, South West Scotland.

In the midst of a worldwide pandemic when the world was in lockdown in 2020 I was part of a poetry book called 'Mother Light' through my training provider Blossom and Berry. The founder, Gayle Berry, suggested making a Mother Light 'mini' series and this is when Family Light: Shining Light on the poetic voices of families was born. The poems in this book have been shared by families throughout lockdown and, as the creator, I have been blown away by the creativity, expression, love, pain and light that has been shared.

www.blossomandberry.com

Acknowledgements

This final poem was written as a special Thanks
to the poets within this book, to read your words,
and feel your feelings and to speak your truth I
say Thank you. Rachel

Family Light

There are poems of love & light
And poems of waiting for new life
There are poems of sadness & the lows
And poems of hopes & dreams
All curated in this book

From birth to teenagers,
And learning to write
Friendships & siblings
Through anxieties & fears, often crippling
Out of darkness, we will fight

Then we have rainbows & moons,
Over our loves that we swoon
Bumpy roads of grief & tears
We have written of sadness & fears

Children with labels & delays
There has been loss, poets in pain
Growing pains & coming to terms
With loss, with connection & mental health

We opened our notebooks & our hearts
To speak our truth before we part
We scribbled & scrambled our brains
We worried of judgement, should we refrain

But our writings are out there now
For all to read, they will all say wow
What a collection, from deep in your hearts
How are you all so full of art

Families in despair, needing a break or in repair
From a pandemic, a lockdown, so unfair
But from the darkness through the night
We hold onto a beacon of Family Light

Rachel Kirkpatrick

Thank you to all the contributors from the land of 'small business' and charities.

Shelley Gibson – Little Lionhearts Childcare
www.facebook.com/LittleLionhearts

Tracey Allen – Made for Little Feet
www.facebook.com/madeforangeldonaghadee

Kerrie McKinnel – Writer
www.kerriemckinnel.com

Candice Torley – Your Zen Birth
www.instagram.com/yourzenbirth

Emma Cottam – Isabella & Us
www.isabellaandus.com
www.facebook.com/isabellaandUs
www.instagram.com/isabella_and_us
www.twitter.com/Isabella_and_us

Mary Atkinson – The Story Massage Programme
www.facebook.com/storymassage
www.storymassage.co.uk

Karen Gibb – Mind Marvels
www.mindmarvels.co.uk
www.instagram.com/mindmarvels

Catherine Jackson – Wise Owls Nursery & Peaceful Pregnancy
www.wiseowlsnurserymoffat.com
Facebook: wise owls nursery and out of school care
Facebook: Peaceful Pregnancy Dumfries & Galloway

Lauren Brydson & Lynsi Mills – D&G Baby Loss Awareness
Simbacharity.org.uk
Facebook: D&G Baby Loss Awareness

Lifelong Learning Team Dumfries & Galloway
Facebook: lifelong learning, Dumfries & Galloway council

Liz Binks – Children's books marketer & publicist
www.instagram.com/lizzies_ditties
Twitter: @lizbinks

Nicola Cloherty – Living in sync with your female monthly cycle
www.instagram.com/nicolacloherty
SELFISH. Podcast

A special thank you to my partner, best friend and family for their patience and support throughout life.

The profits from this book will go to the Scottish Association for Mental Health (Scottish Charity: SC-008897) who support adults and young people with mental health struggles through social care support, services in primary care, schools & further education and have needed much support throughout 2020.

This book will also raise money for various other charities through raffles/fundraisers to spread love, light and support as far as we can as a collective.

Rachel Kirkpatrick – Rose Wellbeing Therapies
www.rosewtherapies.co.uk
Facebook: Rose Wellbeing Therapies
Instagram: @rosewtherapies

I think it's beautiful how a star's light travels the universe, long after it dies. That's what I want to be in this world ~
Someone whose light lingers long after I'm gone.

~John Mark Green

Printed in Poland
by Amazon Fulfillment
Poland Sp. z o.o., Wrocław

61587083R00073